Understandin ZOO ANIMALS

Rosamund Kidman Cox

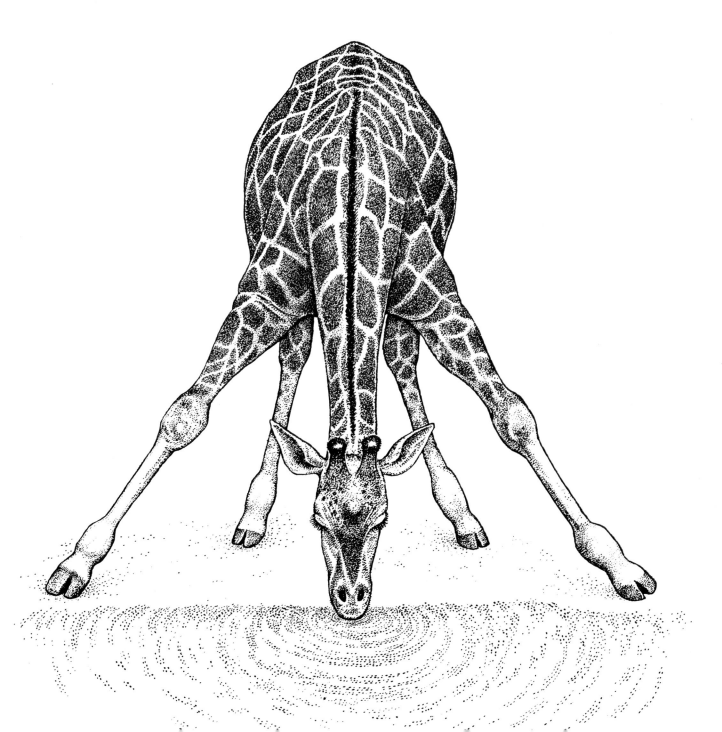

First published in 1980 by
Usborne Publishing Ltd,
20 Garrick Street,
London WC2

© 1980 by Usborne Publishing Ltd.

Giraffe

African Elephant

Illustrated by
Graham Allen, David Astin,
Bob Hersey, David Hurrell,
Gray Jolliffe, Andy Martin,
Malcolm McGregor,
Robert Morton, David Parry,
Phil Weare

Edited by
Rosamund Kidman Cox and
Barbara Cork

Consultant Editor
Miranda Stevenson
of The Royal Zoological
Society of Scotland

Designed by
Sally Burrough

Additional Photography by
Ross & Saczek

Printed in Belgium by
Henri Proost, Turnhout,
Belgium.

Water Buffalo

Grant's Zebra

Understanding ZOO ANIMALS

About this book

This book explains what goes on behind the scenes in a zoo. It tells you what the animals need to keep them healthy and happy and what the keeper does to look after them. There are examples of the sort of animal behaviour that you may see at a zoo, and lots of ideas for things to do when you are on a visit. There is also a special section about releasing zoo animals into the wild, as well as photos from interesting zoos all over the world.

Contents

Impala

Acknowledgements

We would particularly like to thank the staff of the following zoos and organizations for their valuable help and assistance:

Howletts Zoo Park and Port Lympne Wildlife Sanctuary.
The Zoological Society of London.
The Norfolk Wildlife Park.
The North of England Zoological Society, Chester.
The Fauna Preservation Society.
Honolulu Zoo.
Basle Zoological Gardens (Jörg Hess-Haeser).
Birdland Zoo Gardens.
The New England Aquarium.
The New York Zoological Society.
ISIS (Minnesota Zoo).

Going to a zoo

Every distinctly different kind of animal you see at a zoo is a particular "species". For example, the Giant Panda is one species, and the Red Panda (see page 8) is another. Once you can recognize and name some of the different species, start to watch them more closely. This book contains lots of information to help you understand their behaviour.

Some zoos look after their animals better than others, so compare the zoos that you visit and try to judge for yourself whether the animals are happy.

Finding out about the animals

Decide which are your favourite species. Try to read about them before you go so that you know something about their habits. When you get to the zoo, buy a zoo catalogue; this will give you some general information.

GIANT PANDA
Ailuropoda melanoleuca

Carnivora

Each enclosure in the zoo will have a label. This will tell you the English name and the Latin name of the species, the Latin name of the group of animals it belongs to, and where it lives in the wild.

Some zoos have "talking labels". These are machines with a recorded message giving you information about the species and its behaviour.

Preparing for your visit

Decide which zoo to visit (your local library should have a book listing the zoos in your area).

Telephone the zoo to find out opening times. The best time to visit is in the morning when the zoo first opens; many animals are most active then and you will see the keepers at work. Other species are most active in the late afternoon, so this is also a good time to go.

Take a notebook and pencil and a camera if you have one. A cassette tape-recorder is useful if you want to record the animals' voices.

One easy project is to make a study of a particular species. Every time you visit a zoo, note down what you see your animals doing.

Taking photos is the best way to record behaviour, but you can also do rough sketches. Make a scrapbook about the species with your notes and photos.

Taking photographs

Try to photograph the animal in a "natural" setting without any people or barriers in the way. (A lot of the photos in natural history books are taken in zoos). Don't use a flash if the animal is nervous; it may get frightened and hurt itself by running into something.

If there is glass in the way, avoid reflections by putting your camera up against the glass. If you are allowed to go close to a wire-netting barrier, put your camera lens against one of the holes. Watch out for birds pecking at the lens and monkeys trying to snatch your camera.

If you cannot take a photo through a hole in the netting, try to take it so that the wire does not hide the animal's eyes – this will spoil your picture. Don't bother to photograph animals at the far end of a paddock, they will look like tiny dots in your picture.

People-watching

TELL THE KEEPER IF YOU SEE · · · ·

· · SOMEONE TEASING AN ANIMAL

· · SOMEONE THROWING OBJECTS

· · · SOMETHING METAL OR PLASTIC IN THE ENCLOSURE . THE ANIMAL MAY EAT IT AND DIE

Good zoos

Good zoos try to keep their animals in suitable enclosures. The public can then see them behaving naturally and the zoo scientists can study their behaviour. Ideally, zoos should not keep animals unless they intend to breed from them. Good zoos often keep breeding groups of rare species; if it was necessary, they could release some of their animals into the wild.

Unfortunately there are still some zoos that do not look after their animals properly. The bear in the photo above has nothing to do in its small cage; it spends most of its time begging extra food from the public.

Breeding

This baby Tapir was bred in Jersey Zoo (G.B.). Good zoos are building up breeding groups of rare species, so that if a species becomes extinct in the wild, there will at least be some animals left in captivity.

Education

The Wildfowl Trust, Slimbridge (G.B.) has guided tours, and lectures and films about its birds. If people get interested in the animals they see in zoos, they may start to care about the future of animals left in the wild.

Research

These Rockhopper Penguins are being studied at Edinburgh Zoo (G.B.). If a zoo knows about the behaviour of its animals, it can give them suitable enclosures and the right conditions for breeding.

Releasing zoo animals

The Otter Trust (G.B.) is trying to release some of its otters into the wild. Releasing animals is always difficult as a watch must be kept on them, and the release area has to be protected in some way.

The ideal enclosure

This picture shows the sort of conditions zoos should give their animals to keep them healthy and occupied. Although zoo animals have lost their freedom, they are protected from the dangers of the wild – starvation, disease and the risk of being killed by other animals.

Shelter and warmth are provided, plus a quiet place for the female to have her young.

The enclosure has barriers to keep the animals safe from people and other animals.

Animals that live in groups are given companions of the right age and sex. This group of Coatis is made up of females and young.

The animals have things to do to stop them getting bored; for example, these Coatis have branches to climb.

The animals are given the right kind of space; for example, these Coatis have earth for digging. Other animals may need room for flying and jumping, or water to swim in.

The keeper provides food, water and medical aid.

Ring-tailed Coati

Enclosures

Many zoos have only a small amount of space, but they can still give their animals enclosures that allow them to behave naturally. Small enclosures, full of activity equipment, are better than large, empty enclosures where the animals have nothing to do.

You can often tell what sort of enclosure an animal should have by looking at its body. If it has wings, it should have room to fly about. If it has webbed feet, it should have an area of water to swim in. If it has digging-claws, it should have a digging area.

Barriers

Barriers should be high enough to stop even a frightened animal jumping out. They should have no dangerous bits of wire or wood sticking out into the enclosures. Armoured glass is a good barrier to use for monkeys and apes as it protects them from infections. Steel netting is also good as many animals get exercise by climbing it.

Moats are often used instead of fences, but they must be wide enough to stop an animal jumping across, and deep enough to stop it wading across. Most moats have one sloping bank so that if an animal falls in, it can climb out again. Dry moats usually have a safety net

at the bottom. If the animal can swim, like these Polar Bears from Berlin Zoo (W. Germany), or if the moat freezes in winter, then there must be a second barrier such as an electric fence.

Surfaces

Hoofed animals, such as this Black Rhino from Port Lympne (G.B.), are quite happy to spend the whole day feeding. However, if they are in a small paddock, the grass will get very muddy and covered with dung, so it

needs to be renewed every so often. Other hoofed animals, especially mountain animals, such as these Barbary Sheep from London Zoo (G.B.), need hard surfaces to wear down their hooves. Many jungle animals

need climbing structures. This Leopard from Howletts Zoo (G.B.) spends most of its time off the ground. Other animals, like lorises, are actually afraid to walk on the ground, and spend all their time up in the branches.

Water

Many hoofed animals, such as this Water Buffalo, need a daily water or mud bath to keep their skin healthy. Hippos spend most of their time in water and need a large pool. Their water must be changed daily to keep it clean.

Otter pens at The Otter Trust (G.B.) have river water flowing through them. Each pen has a dry sleeping box with a tunnel entrance. As the otter pushes through the tunnel, excess water is squeezed out of its coat.

Many animals may not need water in their enclosures, but do enjoy the occasional swim. The Tiger enclosures at Howletts Zoo (G.B.) contain pools that the Tigers can swim in during the summer months.

Keeping animals occupied

Activities

Banded Mongoose

Zoo animals get bored if they cannot do the things that they would normally do in the wild. Intelligent animals, such as mongooses, are playful and will keep themselves occupied if they have lots of obstacles to run over and around. Small pieces of cage equipment are also important, for example wooden posts for rhinos to rub their horns on and scratching posts for cats.

This Gorilla enclosure at Howletts Zoo (G.B.) has lots of equipment to keep the animals occupied. Highly intelligent animals, such as these dolphins from Whipsnade Zoo (G.B.), will become bored and ill if they are left to swim around their pools, so most zoos occupy them with games or training.

Playing with the keeper

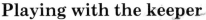

African Elephant

Many animals look forward to the keeper's visits to feed them or clean their enclosures. The elephants know when it is bath time. They enjoy being with the keeper and often make a game out of being hosed down or having their backs scrubbed.

Unnatural behaviour

An animal that does not get enough exercise and has not got enough to do cannot behave naturally. It starts to repeat the few actions that it can still perform until they become a habit.

This bear has developed the habit of pacing endlessly up and down. Bored monkeys or parrots may make a habit of grooming themselves or each other; this often gives them bald patches.

Behaviour games

A large area of the Panaewa Rainforest Zoo in Hawaii has been made into a jungle exhibit for Tigers and gibbons.

The zoo has computerized "games" to stimulate natural behaviour in the animals in exchange for food rewards. There is a model squirrel that the Tigers can chase and "kill" and other devices that encourage jumping and movement. The photo shows one of the Tigers leaping onto a bank to investigate an electronically-made noise.

A mini computer and television screen in the public viewing area provide information on the progress of the "games" and allow the public to activate them.

Territory

Many species hold a territory. This is an area which a group of animals (or one animal) chooses to live in. It is large enough to provide them with food, water and shelter. The animals mark out invisible boundaries with scent from special glands or the scent of dung or urine. They defend these boundaries against rival animals of the same species.

Most animals make their territories feel and smell familiar with frequent scent marking. They feel most secure in their central resting places and least secure near the boundaries.

In a zoo, most species use the enclosure as their territory and the barriers as the boundaries. A zoo territory does not have to be large if the animals do not have to search for food, but there must be room for them to retreat from the boundaries to a quiet resting place. Most zoo animals soon start to feel secure near the boundaries; however, if they are taken outside the enclosure where everything looks and smells unfamiliar, they become very nervous.

Temporary territories

These rival males are having a head-pushing contest.

Uganda Kob

Most hoofed animals cannot hold a proper territory because they are always on the move in search of food. However, in the breeding season, the males of some species, such as the Uganda Kob, hold temporary territories. They try to attract females into these areas for mating. Mock fights often occur between rival males.

Zoos must be careful not to keep too many males with the females in a small space; if they do, serious fighting will occur.

Scent marking

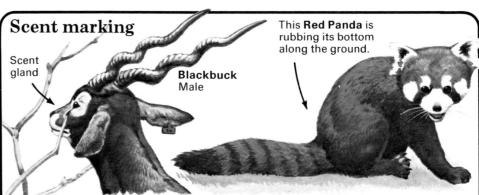

Scent gland

Blackbuck Male

This Red Panda is rubbing its bottom along the ground.

This antelope is not having a scratch; it is leaving its scent mark on a twig. Watch carefully if you see an animal rubbing itself against something in its enclosure – it could be leaving a scent mark.

Scent glands may be on any part of the body. This Panda is using glands on its bottom. The keeper must be careful not to clean all an animal's enclosure in case he removes its smell and makes the animal feel insecure.

Family territories

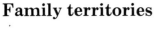

When the **Siamang Gibbon** hoots, its throat swells up.

Gibbon families hold territories; they warn away rival families by hooting. Many bird families hold a territory in the breeding season, when the young need food and shelter.

Ocelot Male

Slow Loris

Male cats use urine to leave scent marks. You will often see them spraying the barriers. The Hippopotamus uses dung to mark the trails in its territory; it vibrates its tail to spread the dung over a large area.

Lorises, some lemurs and some South American monkeys put urine on their paws and then wipe them on branches to leave scent marks. This Slow Loris is about to wipe some of its urine onto the branch.

Temperature and light

In the wild, some animals need a change of temperature or light during the year to get them to breed. Zoos often encourage breeding by altering the light or temperature inside an enclosure.

Zoo animals all need warm, dry, quiet sleeping quarters that they can enter at any time. Bad zoos close off the sleeping quarters during opening hours to make sure the animals are always on view. Hoofed animals need stalls to go into at night or to shelter in during bad weather.

Warmth

Suricate Meerkat

Tigers do not mind the snow.

Species from hot climates, like these Meerkats (related to mongooses), often like to bask under the warmth of a sun lamp. Most species from hot climates do not mind going outside in cold weather so long as they have a warm area to go back to. In very hot weather, the keeper may use a water hose to cool down animals from colder climates, such as the penguins.

The nocturnal house

None of the nocturnal (night-living) animals can see in total darkness, so in the wild they are active at dawn, dusk, or when the moon is out. In zoos, they are put together in a nocturnal house. During the daytime, the enclosure lighting is very low; the animals think that it is night and come out to feed. Red, green or blue lights may be used because most nocturnal animals cannot see these colours well. At night, white lights are turned on so that the animals think it is daytime and go to sleep. The photo below shows a Palm Civet in the nocturnal house at Frankfurt Zoo (W. Germany).

Special senses

Bushbaby

Springhaas

Solenodon

Each nocturnal animal has one or more of its senses highly developed to help it find its way around at night. Look at the animals in the nocturnal house and try to guess which of their senses they use most. Some have large eyes to make full use of all the available light. Others have sensitive noses and whiskers to help them feel their way about, or large ears to improve their hearing.

Bats have very special hearing. They make high-pitched noises through their noses or mouths. The sound is reflected off objects (such as insects) in their path and the bats pick up the echoes with their sensitive ears. In this way they can "see" in the dark.

Homes in water

At Edinburgh Zoo (G.B.), Gentoo Penguins and King Penguins are kept in the same enclosure. In the wild, penguins are found in large breeding colonies, so the zoo keeps them in big groups. Once baby penguins reach a certain age, they are moved to another enclosure to prevent over-crowding. The King Penguins have to be fed by hand as they refuse to pick up fish lying on the ground. The keeper also feeds the Gentoos by hand; he can then make sure that each bird has enough to eat.

The penguin pool at Edinburgh Zoo

King Penguin parents take it in turns to rest the single egg on their feet; they keep it covered with a fold of skin.

Eight-month old King Penguin.

Chicks are covered with down.

Preening strengthens the friendship between a pair.

Whales and dolphins

This Killer Whale is from Vancouver Aquarium (Canada). Whales and dolphins are very intelligent marine mammals. Their pools must contain sea water or salted water; it has to be changed regularly to keep it clean. If dolphins are kept in fresh water, their skin will get damaged. Unfortunately, few zoos give whales and dolphins enough space for breeding, so you are unlikely to see young ones.

Gentoo Penguins

The male and female take turns to sit on the eggs. The returning bird greets its mate with a trumpeting call.

Gentoos are given pebbles for their nests. The concrete bases are just far enough apart to stop the penguins pecking each other.

Penguins can jump out of the water.

Penguins cannot fly, but use their flippers (wings) as paddles for swimming.

Penguins have a streamlined shape to help them swim fast under water.

Underwater views

These are Harbour Seals from Bergen Aquarium (Norway). This aquarium specializes in northern marine species and gives all its animals fresh sea water. If you find an underwater view of a pool, watch to see how each species swims. Seals swim by moving their hind flippers; sealions swim with their front flippers.

Both parents feed the chick with partly digested food.

Bird houses

The free-flight aviary at London Zoo (G.B.)

The Tropical House at The Wildfowl Trust (G.B.)

A lot of zoos have bird houses (aviaries) where many different species are kept together. The birds have a large area of flying space, plus a choice of natural nesting materials and nest sites.

Tropical birds are usually kept in indoor houses where the daylight can be artificially lengthened and the birds can be given a moist atmosphere to keep their feathers in good condition. Birds do not like flying into dark areas, so the public walk-way through a tropical house is often in semi-darkness.

Aggressive species and the meat-eaters, such as the birds of prey (hawks, eagles and vultures), are housed on their own. They have a large wing-span and need lots of space for their courtship displays. They may also need a quiet nest area away from the public.

Feeding

Rainbow Bee-eater

Birds that need live food are difficult to feed in zoos. This Bee-eater feeds in flight; it needs a daily supply of live insects.

The Kiwi cannot fly.

Nostrils

The Kiwi feeds at night on live earthworms. It can smell them with its nostrils which are at the end of its long, probing beak.

Preening

Fischer's Lovebird

Nests

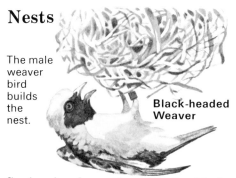

The male weaver bird builds the nest.

Black-headed Weaver

Spring is a busy time for the bird keepers as this is when most of the birds are nesting. Weaver birds must be given grass for their nests and branches to hang them from. They are kept in groups and all

Burrowing Owl

build their nests on the same tree. Some birds need unusual nesting places. In the wild, Burrowing Owls often use the burrows of other animals. In zoos, they may be given a pipe to nest in.

Birds preen their feathers every day. Lovebirds often perch close together and preen each other. They fluff out their feathers and straighten each one with their beaks. They also waterproof their feathers by spreading oil on them from glands under their wings or tail.

The reptile house

The reptile house is usually run as an independent unit in a zoo. It has its own kitchens and sick room.

A few reptiles are very poisonous, so the reptile house has an alarm system with direct telephone links to a doctor or hospital. The keepers may carry walkie-talkies so they can call each other in an emergency. In most zoos, enclosures are shut off from the public walk-ways by safety doors.

Reptiles (and amphibians) cannot adjust their own body temperature as mammals can. They warm up or cool down by moving in or out of warm areas. In zoos, the enclosures should have hot and cold areas so the animals can move about to adjust their own temperature. Reptiles are most active when they are hot (although they do not like to be too hot); when they are cold, their body activity slows down.

Reptiles from cold climates usually hibernate (go into a deep sleep) when it gets too cold to be active. In zoos, they may not breed if they do not hibernate, so once a year zoos reduce the light and temperature to make them think it is winter.

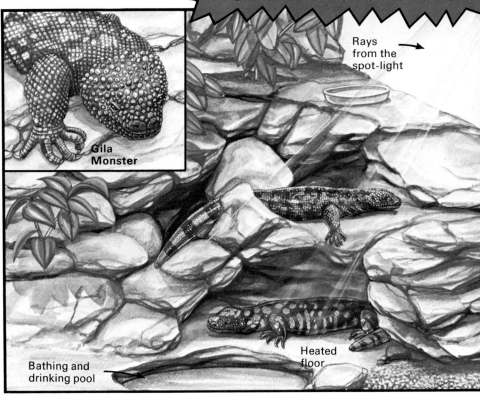

Gila Monster

Rays from the spot-light

Bathing and drinking pool

Heated floor

This is the Gila Monster enclosure in Chester Zoo (G.B.). The floor is heated and the lizards can warm up under the spot-light, or go into one of the cold dens if they become too hot. Strip-lights provide artificial daylight which helps prevent the reptiles developing an illness called rickets.

All the enclosures at Chester Zoo are cleaned every day; this helps prevent disease. At cleaning time, very poisonous species are coaxed into a box at the back of their enclosures.

As a reptile grows and its skin becomes worn, it grows a new one underneath and sheds the old skin; this is called sloughing. You can tell when a reptile is about to slough; its skin (including the skin over its eyes) will look dull and cloudy. To help the skin peel off, it may bathe in its pool and rub against rocks in the enclosure.

Poisonous reptiles

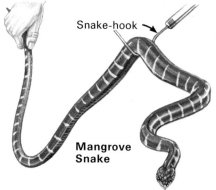

Snake-hook

Mangrove Snake

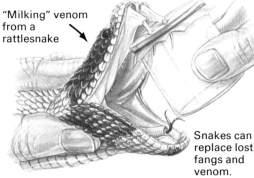

"Milking" venom from a rattlesnake

Snakes can replace lost fangs and venom.

Not all reptiles are dangerous. Many snakes, such as this python, are not poisonous and can be handled. If a poisonous snake has to be moved, it is picked up with a snake-hook, placed on a flat surface and gently held down at the neck with the back of the hook. It can then be grasped behind the head. In case of bites, the zoo (or a nearby hospital) keeps a supply of anti-venom serum – a different serum for each poisonous species. The serum is injected into the victim to stop the venom working.

Snake venom is needed to produce serum, so snakes are "milked" of their venom by being forced to bite a rubber skin stretched over a glass.

Feeding

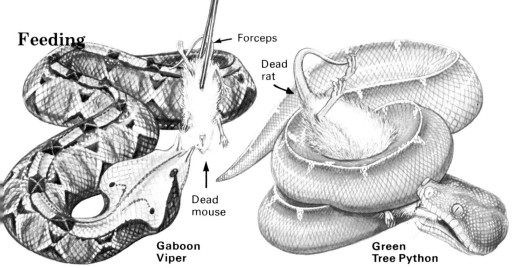

Forceps

Dead rat

Dead mouse

Gaboon Viper

Green Tree Python

Most meat-eating reptiles (depending on their size and how active they are) are given dead animals once or twice a week. Snake food is held in forceps and shaken so that it looks alive. Snakes can smell their food.

Watch to see how the different reptiles feed. Anacondas, boas and pythons constrict (squeeze) their food before eating it. Lizards may use their tongues to pick up food. Tortoises have no teeth; they tear and chew food with their gums.

Amphibians

Tree Frog

Some amphibians (frogs, toads, newts and salamanders) may also be kept in the reptile house. They soak up water through their skins instead of drinking, so their enclosures need to be kept moist.

Breeding

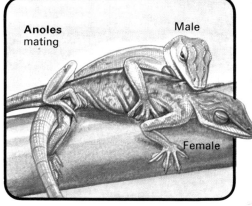

Anoles mating

Male

Female

Male and female reptiles are usually difficult to tell apart. Sometimes the female is larger, or the male is brightly coloured.

Most reptiles lay eggs with soft shells, but some, for example vipers and boas, give birth to live young. When a birth is due, the female is moved to a quiet place. The glass of her enclosure may be painted over so she will not be disturbed. If eggs are laid, she either wraps herself around them or buries them in sand or a nest.

With rare species, where it is important to rear as many young as possible, the keeper may remove the eggs and put them in an incubator. This is a special container which keeps the eggs at exactly the right temperature and humidity (moisture) until they hatch out. Very young reptiles are called hatchlings.

The female **Mississippi Alligator** guards the nest and the young hatchlings. She may attack the keeper if he comes too close.

The Alligator's eggs are buried in the middle of this warm, moist nest. All reptile eggs must be kept moist as they need to take up moisture during incubation.

Rubbery shell

Hatchling

Male reptiles may have mock fights or wrestling matches to decide who will mate with the female. Alligators have roaring matches. They lift themselves out of the water on their front legs, thrash their tails and roar so loudly that their bodies vibrate.

When a female alligator has mated, the keeper gives her grass and mud to make a nest. She buries the eggs inside.

When the babies are ready to hatch they make a cheeping noise. The female hears them and digs up the hatching eggs.

The keeper's job

The keepers are directly in charge of the animals, and in large zoos, scientists (called curators) are responsible for each major group of animals, such as mammals, birds or reptiles.

A director is the head of a zoo. He may employ a business manager, and a supplies manager to order food and equipment. He also employs general staff such as gardeners and workmen.

Keepers usually begin as helpers. A few zoos run training courses, but most keepers learn their job through experience. Much of a keeper's time is spent doing heavy and dirty work like cleaning. The hours are long and a keeper may be called to the zoo at any time in an emergency.

Part of the keeper's duty involves making daily records of any change in the animals' diet, behaviour or housing. Many zoos send the general details about each of their animals, for example births and deaths, to a central computer in America. This computer is used to trace the ancestry of animals and to help the zoos exchange animals for breeding.

Getting to know the animals

Indian Elephant

Woolly Monkey

Monkeys will greet a passing keeper.

Zoo animals are not treated as pets, but relationships often develop between the keeper and his animals. Many recognize him by his face, uniform, or smell, when he enters or passes their enclosures and will greet him with a noise or a movement.

Occasionally adult male animals see the keeper as a rival (usually at mating time) and may be aggressive towards him.

Identification

Hoofed animals that look alike may be marked with numbered ear tags. The colour of the tag may distinguish the males from the females.

Apes can be recognized by their faces.

Birds are marked with numbered leg rings.

Collars are used for marking small monkeys such as marmosets.

Reptiles and amphibians are difficult to mark. Some may have numbers marked on their skin with a freeze-branding needle. Tortoises may have numbers or notches marked on their shells.

Penguins are marked with numbered flipper bands.

Looking at markings

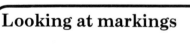

Many animals can be identified by their colours or markings; for example every Tiger has a different pattern of stripes on its face. To help you remember which animal is which, take photos or make reference sketches and keep them with your study notes.

Numbers are marked on some mammals by freeze-branding; this is painless but turns the skin or fur white.

The pictures above show some of the ways of identifying animals. The keeper must be able to identify all his animals so that he can keep accurate records. Animals that have different markings are easy to tell apart, but animals that look exactly alike may be marked with the number that is on their record card.

Moving the animals

Travel boxes must be large enough for an animal to stand up and lie down in, but small enough to stop it turning and perhaps trapping itself.

The floor may be ridged to stop the animal slipping, and the walls may be padded to stop it grazing itself.

Sliding door

New animals are bought from other zoos or from dealers; dealers may get their stock from animal trappers. This zebra has been travelling all day from another zoo. It is frightened to leave the security of its box, so the keepers are trying to coax it out. They have opened the back door so that the zebra comes out backwards instead of rushing out head-first and crashing into the barriers. When the zebra has settled down and started to feed, it will be given a health check and examined for internal parasitic worms. It will then be moved into the main paddock with the other zebras.

Dangerous people

Stealing eggs

Banging on the glass

Cutting the wire

The most dangerous animals in a zoo are people. Much of a keeper's time is spent watching the visitors and stopping them from doing stupid or dangerous things.

Stupid people bang on the barriers to get the animals to move; this just frightens the animals. If snakes are frightened they may hurt their noses by striking at the glass.

More dangerous is the type of person who gets into the enclosure or breaks the barriers. A lot of breeding programmes are ruined by people disturbing nesting animals, or stealing the eggs or young animals.

Bird transport

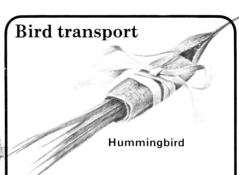
Hummingbird

This hummingbird is going to another zoo. The keeper has fitted it with a jacket to stop it flapping its wings and hurting itself in the travel box. It will need to be kept warm during the journey.

Tragedies

This bear was being sent by an animal dealer in Malaya to a British zoo. The box had not got enough air holes and the bear suffocated on the journey. To prevent tragedies like this, a keeper must make sure that an animal has food and water on a journey and that its box is well ventilated and not too small.

Escapes

Very few animals try to escape. The ones that do get out are the burrowers and gnawers. However, if an animal is badly frightened, it may leap over or break through the barriers. An escaped animal is usually only too glad to return to the security of its enclosure, but sometimes, the keeper has to tempt it back with food, or force it to move by using a water hose.

Very occasionally an animal escapes from the zoo grounds. Usually it is very frightened and makes for the nearest hiding place. The keeper has to find it and coax it into a travel box. If this fails, he will get the vet to dope it with a tranquillizing dart; he will then try to catch it with a net.

A day in the life of a keeper

8:30 Brian Stocks, head cat keeper at Howletts Zoo (G.B.), leaves his house in the zoo grounds to go on his morning rounds.

8:45 He visits all the cats – including the cats in quarantine. These Barbary Lions are being kept in quarantine for six months.

9:10 Bob Wilson, another keeper, has collected some dead animals from a local farm. He cuts them up ready for feeding time.

9:40 The larger cats are fed once or twice a week. Today Brian feeds the Tigers, the Snow Leopards and the Clouded Leopards.

11:00 The cats Brian has reared by hand allow him into their enclosures. He removes the dirt and fills their water dishes.

12:10 The Tigers greet Brian with a snort when he enters their enclosures. This male wants to have a game with his old bone.

12:25 He leaves the last Tiger enclosure, and makes sure both doors are shut. He fits a padlock on the outer door so no-one can get in.

13:45 After lunch, Brian treats one of the tigers for worms. He mixes the medicine with milk and gives it to the Tiger to drink.

14:10 This male Clouded Leopard is Brian's favourite cat. He has mixed some medicine with its milk to help it recover from a bad cold.

If Brian has time, he may play with the cats. Although he has never been bitten, he makes sure another keeper is near in case of accidents.

15:45 There is a pair of Caracal cats in this box. They have been tranquillized by the vet so Brian can move them to a new enclosure.

16:45 His last job is to fill in his daily diary, and note down on the cats' record cards which ones were given medicine today.

16

Illness and the vet

The keeper can usually tell when an animal is unwell by its behaviour or appearance. It may act strangely, lose weight or have an unhealthy-looking coat. The vet's job is to discover what is wrong and to work out how to treat the sick animal. This may be difficult if the animal is dangerous (like a crocodile with tooth-ache) or large (like an elephant).

The vet may also carry out regular health checks on the animals. He will trim any hooves or claws that have grown too long, and will examine the animals' dung for signs of parasites (tiny organisms that feed off an animal).

Big zoos may have a hospital with an X-ray machine, an operating theatre and a quarantine area for new arrivals. Animals in quarantine are isolated so that if they are carrying an infection, they will not give it to other animals. After a death, the vet has to examine the body to find out why the animal died.

Treatment in the hospital

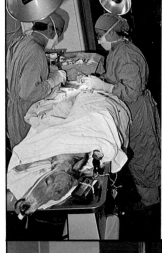
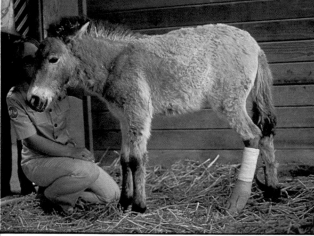

▲ The two photos above are from San Diego Zoo (U.S.). The young Przewalski's Horse fell and broke its leg. The vet gave it a mild anaesthetic to make it dopey and then took it to the operating theatre. He gave it another anaesthetic and then operated to straighten the break. Back in its stall, the horse was given an injection to wake it up. The bandage was left on until the leg mended.

◄ This photo shows a male De Brazza Monkey from Taronga Zoo (Australia) that was bitten in a fight. The vet caught the monkey and took it to the treatment room. Here he gave it an anaesthetic and then cleaned and bandaged its wounds.

Handling the animals

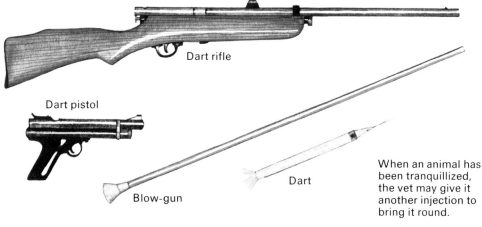

Dart rifle

Dart pistol

Blow-gun

Dart

When an animal has been tranquillized, the vet may give it another injection to bring it round.

When treating an animal, the vet has to find a way to keep it still and prevent it panicking (animals can die from shock). The keeper may hold small mammals and birds while they are being examined. Sometimes animals are placed in a "squeeze cage". This has one wall which slides along the floor of the cage and holds the animal against the opposite side so that it cannot struggle.

If the animal is likely to panic, the vet will make it dopey with a mild anaesthetic. He must know the exact dose to use and where to inject it. When it is not possible to inject by hand, the vet fires the dart with a blow-gun; this is silent and will not frighten the animal. With large mammals (which need a large dose of drug) he will use a pistol.

If he cannot get close to an animal, he will use a rifle to make sure that he fires the dart into the right part of its body.

Feeding

Correct feeding is very important if zoo animals are to be kept healthy and occupied. Many animals will not breed if they do not have a suitable diet. Since zoo animals come from all over the world, it is often too difficult and expensive to give each animal its natural diet. This means that the zoo has to work out alternative diets that contain enough goodness. Sometimes, the important ingredients of a diet are mixed together and given to the animals in a concentrated pellet form.

Buying the supplies

Most zoos have a supplies officer who orders all the food for the animals. The picture below shows you some of the food that is regularly bought for a zoo.

Zoos buy carcasses of horses, sheep or cows. These may be cut up and stored in a deep freeze along with frozen fish.

Many plant-eaters are given branches to eat. Greenery, such as bamboo for Giant Pandas, may come from private gardens.

← Salt lick

Preparing the food

Food rations for the animals are prepared by the keepers.

Clean, good quality hay and bales of clover hay are bought from wholesale merchants. Dried, fresh grass may be bought in pellet form. Grain, rice, nuts and dog biscuits are bought in bulk.

Some food is bought in tins and jars. For example, meat for the smaller mammals and vitamin and mineral powder for all the animals. Tins of baby food and powdered milk are used for young animals that have to be reared by hand.

Concentrated pellet food is bought for many of the animals. Hoofed animals have horse cubes or herbivore pellets; some amphibians have trout pellets; monkeys have primate pellets.

Fruit and vegetables are bought fresh from the nearest market or wholesaler. Small zoos often have their own greenhouses and grow their own vegetables.

Baby mouse

Mealworm

Locust

Some animals are fed flies, worms and locusts; others are fed on dead mice or rats. All these animals may be bred in the zoo.

DO NOT FEED ZOO ANIMALS

Balanced diet for
RUFFED LEMUR :
20% Monkey pellets
50% Fruit
25% Vegetables
5% Eggs, milk
and extras

Zoo animals are given the correct amount of food containing the right mixture of nourishing ingredients. If you feed the animals, you will upset their balanced diets.

Bear begging for food

The keepers encourage the animals to take exercise by putting food at various points in their enclosures. Animals fed by the public tend to stand in one spot begging for food and do not get enough exercise.

Feeding places

Proboscis Monkey

Some tree-climbing animals, such as this Proboscis Monkey, prefer to eat their food off the ground; the keeper usually puts their food up on a shelf. If there are any shy animals in a group he may have to feed them on their own.

Overweight elephant

Extra feeding by the public makes the animals fat and constipated; too much sweet food gives them tooth decay. Zoo animals may also catch infections from food that has been handled by people.

The keepers make sure that all the animals, not just the bossy ones, get their fair share of food. Extra feeding by the public often causes fights among the animals.

Drinking water

Drinking nozzle

Squirrel Monkey

Water and food dishes must be clean to prevent disease spreading. This drinking nozzle provides fresh water when the monkey sucks it. Water troughs are filled automatically; they may have covers to stop dirt getting in.

Chewing and gnawing

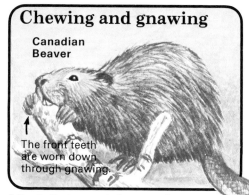

Canadian Beaver

The front teeth are worn down through gnawing.

Most diets contain roughage, such as plant fibres or bones, to keep the animals' jaw and gut muscles exercised. Some species have teeth that need to be worn down; these animals must be given something hard to gnaw on.

Keeping the animals occupied

Lowland Gorilla

Many animals, particularly the plant-eaters, spend hours in the wild foraging (searching) for food. Most zoos cannot give their animals enough space for foraging; instead they try to make their diets as interesting as possible. They

may sprinkle nuts or grain around their enclosures to keep them occupied feeding. At Howletts Zoo (G.B.) the ape keeper sprinkles food in amongst the straw; looking for the food keeps the Gorillas busy for hours.

Watching feeding

Looking at mouths

If you look at an animal's mouth when it is feeding or yawning you can often tell quite accurately the type of food it eats. Note down all the clues, then have a guess.

BABOON
Teeth easy to see.
mixed feeder?

canines (for fighting?)
grinders
nippers

AFRICAN BUFFALO
No upper teeth
Herbivore

KILLER WHALE
Many sharp teeth.
Carnivore

Does the shape of the mouth or lips suggest anything? Has it got a long tongue? Does it have rows of sharp, cutting teeth, or rows of flat-topped, grinding teeth? Are there any long, dagger-shaped canine teeth (used for feeding or fighting)? What food is in the enclosure?

A mixed feeder

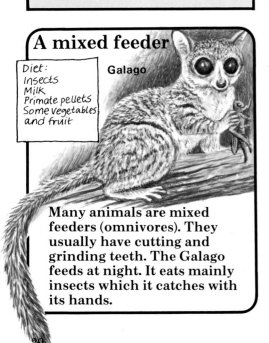

Galago

Diet:
Insects
Milk
Primate pellets
Some vegetables
and fruit

Many animals are mixed feeders (omnivores). They usually have cutting and grinding teeth. The Galago feeds at night. It eats mainly insects which it catches with its hands.

A meat-eater

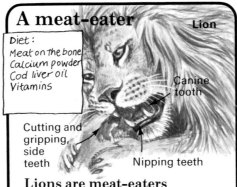

Lion

Diet:
Meat on the bone
Calcium powder
Cod liver oil
Vitamins

Canine tooth

Cutting and gripping side teeth

Nipping teeth

Lions are meat-eaters (carnivores). Meat is very nourishing, so most large carnivores do not need a meal every day. They are given meat on the bone to exercise their jaws.

An insect-eater

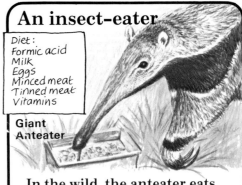

Diet:
Formic acid
Milk
Eggs
Minced meat
Tinned meat
Vitamins

Giant Anteater

In the wild, the anteater eats termites (ant-like insects). It digs them out of their nests with its front claws and picks them up with its long, sticky tongue. It has no teeth.

Plant-eaters

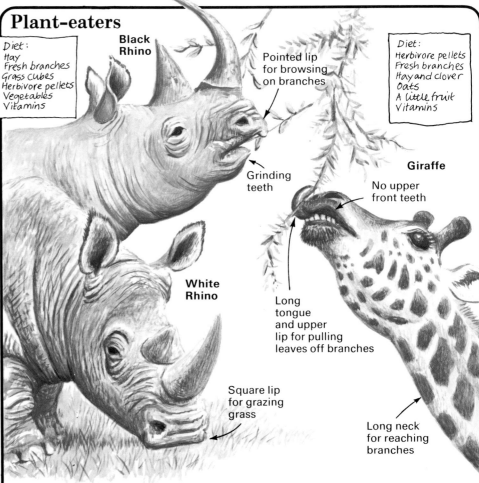

Black Rhino

Diet:
Hay
Fresh branches
Grass cubes
Herbivore pellets
Vegetables
Vitamins

Pointed lip for browsing on branches

Grinding teeth

White Rhino

Square lip for grazing grass

Diet:
Herbivore pellets
Fresh branches
Hay and clover
Oats
A little fruit
Vitamins

Giraffe

No upper front teeth

Long tongue and upper lip for pulling leaves off branches

Long neck for reaching branches

Plant material contains lots of indigestible fibre; plant-eaters (herbivores) must eat lots of plants to get enough goodness from them. Large, powerful animals such as rhinos, stew plants for a long time in their stomachs. Some hoofed animals such as Giraffes, cattle and deer, get the goodness from plants by "chewing the cud"; they chew and swallow their food, then bring it up again for a second chew.

Looking at hands, feet and beaks

If you see any animals being fed, jot down in your notebook how they use their hands, feet, or beaks to handle their food.

BROWN BEAR (Right paw) Dug up earth with claws, possibly looking for grubs.

ORANG UTAN (Left foot) Can pick up food with its feet.

OSPREY Hooked beak used for tearing flesh while fish held by long claws. (claws pierced flesh)

Primates (apes, monkeys, lemurs and tree shrews) have sensitive fingers for picking up and holding food. A hoof may be useful for scraping up roots. Claws can be used to dig up, or tear food. Beaks are specially shaped for different methods of feeding. For example, finches have thick, strong beaks for crushing seeds, and pelicans have large, wide beaks with pouches for scooping fish out of the water.

Using hands and feet

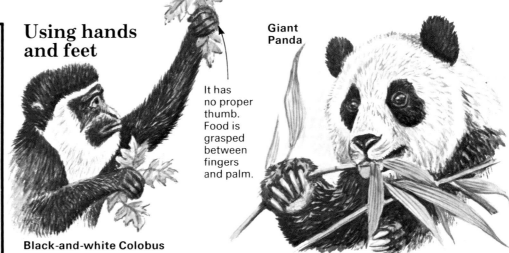

It has no proper thumb. Food is grasped between fingers and palm.

Black-and-white Colobus

Giant Panda

The Colobus comes from the rainforests of Africa. It feeds on leaves in the tree tops, so in zoos, branches are usually placed off the ground. It eats a lot of leaves and has a large stomach to digest them.

The Giant Panda's natural diet is bamboo. The pads on the palms and toes of its front feet are flexible so that it can hold the bamboo stems. In zoos, it is also fed on milk, monkey pellets and some vegetables.

In the wild, the Dwarf Mongoose eats small animals; it also uses its front paws to search for food. Its zoo diet includes meat, insects and some fruit. It likes eggs and will pick them up with its paws and smash them on the floor. It may drink by dipping its paw into water and licking it.

Claws

Dwarf Mongoose

Palm Cockatoo

It can pick up food with its feet.

The Palm Cockatoo is fed on seeds, nuts, some leaves and vegetables; food is placed on a stand off the ground. It has the most powerful beak of any parrot and can crack open any nut.

Special diets

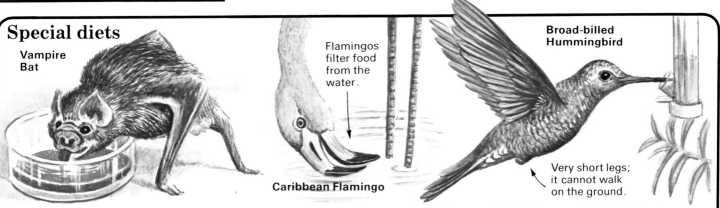

Vampire Bat

Flamingos filter food from the water.

Caribbean Flamingo

Broad-billed Hummingbird

Very short legs; it cannot walk on the ground.

The Vampire drinks a quarter of a litre of fresh blood a day. The blood comes from a slaughter house; vitamins are added, plus a chemical to stop the blood clotting.

In the wild, flamingos and other pink or red birds eat plants containing natural chemicals called pigments that make their feathers red. In zoos, these pigments are added to their food.

Adult hummingbirds feed on the wing, sucking nectar from flowers with their long tongues. Zoos prepare a nectar solution from honey, or grape sugar and vitamins.

Studying behaviour

Zoos are good places to study behaviour as you can get close to the animals. However, if an enclosure is not very good, some of the animals' behaviour may be unnatural (see page 7). Many zoos have clubs that can help you if you want to make a serious study of a zoo animal.

Most animals signal some of their feelings to other animals by movements and body positions (body language). If you study a species that lives in groups, for example the wolf, you will see a lot of body language.

Groups of animals usually have a boss and the other animals are arranged in order of importance under him or her. This is called a chain of dominance or rank order and the boss is called the top rank animal. High rank animals signal their dominance (superiority) to animals of lower rank. Low rank animals may allow dominant animals to take away their food or mates — this is called submissive behaviour.

Canadian Timber Wolf

Wolves are very playful. They greet friends by tail wagging, licking and jumping up.

Top rank male

High rank wolf

She is signalling that she is dominant by snarling and staring at the other wolf. Her ears and tail are up.

High rank wolves mark the pack's territory with scent.

This low rank wolf is signalling with her body language that she is submissive (she is exposing her belly, her ears are back and her tail is between her legs). These signals will stop the dominant wolf attacking.

When one wolf starts to howl, the others join in. They howl to warn away rival packs from their territory. Howling is most common when the pups are young or if food is nearby.

The top male mates with the top female. She is usually the only wolf to have pups.

When the pups stop suckling milk, they are fed with partly digested food. All the wolves help to look after them.

Pups are lower in rank than adults. They have their own rank order.

Many zoos keep packs of wolves in a small area of woodland. A large pack has a male and a female rank order. The top rank male and the top rank female will be large, healthy wolves.

The rank order of the wolves will change from time to time. However, you can recognize a low rank wolf by its hunched walk, with tail down and ears back. High rank wolves hold their head, ears and tails up.

Monkeys and apes

You will see a lot of interesting behaviour if you choose to study monkeys or apes. Unlike other mammals, they have a poor sense of smell. They make up for this by having good sight. Instead of leaving scent messages, they use face expressions, body language and calls to communicate.

Most mammals see in black and white, but monkeys and apes see in colour. This helps them recognize their food by sight rather than smell. Some monkeys use coloured skin around their sex organs to attract partners for mating.

The most colourful monkey is a male Mandrill. His colours attract females and warn away rival males. The colours on his bottom are repeated on his face to make the message more obvious.

Grooming

Grooming and touching is comforting and a way of saying "I want to be friendly". Low rank animals groom their superiors and a high rank animal may groom a low rank animal to reassure it.

This high rank male is threatening a low rank male with an anger display. He is making himself look fierce by banging things and yelling.

This male is punishing a cheeky youngster.

Anger expression

His fur is standing on end.

Chimps are very intelligent. This one is using a stick as a tool to poke out some food.

Fear expression

This low rank Chimp is signalling that he is submissive by showing his bottom to the high rank Chimp.

Watching faces

Pout face (Chimp): ▶ greeting a friend or wanting something.

◀ Play face (Chimp): Lower teeth show.

Fear grin (Chimp): ▶ All the teeth are exposed; it may also scream.

◀ Threat and anger (baboon): exposing long, fighting canine teeth.

Threat-stare (mangabey): ▶ staring and flashing its eyelids.

◀ Friendly face (macaque): the teeth chatter and the lips move up and down.

Apes and monkeys have very expressive faces. The same face expression may be used with different body signals to express different moods.

Breeding

Zoos try to breed their animals so they can supply other zoos with animals or build up large numbers of rare species.

Some animals do not breed well in zoos, usually because they are kept in the wrong conditions. For successful breeding, zoos must know when an animal is mature (ready to breed) and when it is in season (ready to mate).

Many animals need a lot of space for courtship or nesting. Others need special lighting or heating to encourage them to breed. With most species, the number of animals kept together is also important. Until recently, zoos failed to breed Cheetahs because they got this mixture wrong.

Courtship behaviour

Indian Sarus Crane

Cranes have a courtship dance. They leap up and down together making loud cries.

The male **Indian Peafowl** is brilliantly coloured during the breeding season.

When a peacock wants to court a peahen, he opens up his long feathers and rattles them in front of her. She will choose him if he gives a good display.

An animal attracts a mate by a special series of body movements or noises. This behaviour conveys the message: "I am of the same species, I am a male/female, I am friendly, I am ready to mate".

Usually the male is the most active partner during courtship. He may bring the female food as an offering, display his size or colouring, or fight in front of her to show his strength. The male may also have to win a territory before he can attract a female. However, sometimes the female is the most active partner in courtship. She may play in front of the male, or try to attract him by repeatedly approaching him and then running away.

Spring is the best time to see courtship behaviour in a zoo. If an animal has several mates during each breeding season, courtship is usually short, but if a pair stay together for the season, or for life, then the courtship takes longer. Sarus Cranes pair for life; their long courtship strengthens the bond of friendship between them.

Rival males

Red Kangaroo

Rival kangaroos have boxing matches.

Red Kangaroos can mate at any time of the year. The males have boxing matches to decide who will mate with the females. Grey Kangaroos have a breeding season once a year; rival males compete for the females in the spring.

Introducing a mate

Chimpanzee

Female chimps have swollen bottoms when they are in season.

A male will sniff a female's bottom to see if she is ready to mate.

Female chimps are kept with the males. They come into season every month unless they are pregnant. With other species, for example beavers, the female is kept on her own until she is mature. When she comes into season, the keeper introduces a male. If the two like each other they will pair for life. However, the keeper must keep watch in case they do not get on together and start to fight.

Getting ready to mate

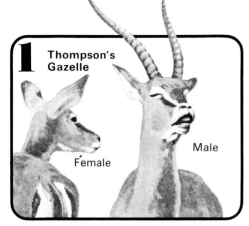

A male Gazelle will smell or taste a female's urine to see if she is in season. After doing this, he lifts his upper lip and pulls a face. If she is in season, he signals to her that he wants to mate by drumming his feet on the ground and following close behind her. Finally, he will ask her permission by tapping her back leg with his front foot. If she does not move off, he mates with her.

A male Kudu asks a female to mate with him by laying his head on her neck or back. Hoofed animals usually mate quickly because, in the wild, they are always in danger of being attacked by other animals.

Mating

When carnivores mate, the male holds the female gently by her neck. This is the same hold that they use to kill prey, so the female must not struggle in case the male bites her by mistake and kills her. When they part, the female may growl and hit out at the male to drive him away.

The birth

The Hippo carries her newborn baby on her muzzle.

The Hippo gives birth to its baby in the water. Most large mammals have a long pregnancy and give birth to one or two babies in the open. These babies can see and are able to walk or swim almost at once. Small mammals have a short pregnancy and give birth to several babies in a nest. It may be a few weeks before the babies can see or walk, but they are safe while they are in the nest. Tell the keeper if you see an animal being born; he may need to call the vet.

Preparing for the birth

The Tree Shrew needs two nest boxes; she sleeps in one and leaves her babies in another.

Some mothers, like this Tree Shrew, need a second nest box for their babies. Other mothers need a choice of nesting places. If the keeper knows when the female mated, he will know when the birth is due and can make the necessary preparations.

Just before the birth, the female's behaviour changes. She may become restless and stop feeding; her nipples become swollen and she may lick her bottom.

Parents and young

Eggs

Platypus

The air in an incubator is kept warm and moist.

Only two mammals lay eggs – the Echidna and the Platypus. The Platypus lays two eggs which she keeps warm and moist until they hatch. She squeezes milk from pores on her stomach and the babies lick it off her fur.

If a keeper wants to rear a lot of chicks, he can get some birds to lay more eggs by removing the first clutch. He will artificially hatch these eggs in an incubator while the bird is hatching the second clutch of eggs.

The first hours

Axis or **Spotted Deer**

The mother is licking the birth sac off her newborn baby.

Newborn babies are covered in a transparent birth sac which the mother licks off. In the first few hours, the mother learns to recognize the smell of her baby, and the baby, once its eyes are open, learns to recognize the sight and smell of its mother. A baby reared by hand will see the keeper as its mother. When it grows up it may refuse to mate with members of its own species.

Animals with pouches

Most marsupials come from Australia. They have a fold of skin on their stomachs called a pouch. Newborn babies are tiny, naked and blind. They climb up their mother's fur from the base of her tail into her pouch; here they attach themselves to a nipple.

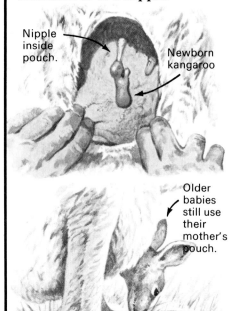

Nipple inside pouch.

Newborn kangaroo

Older babies still use their mother's pouch.

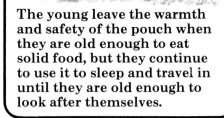

The young leave the warmth and safety of the pouch when they are old enough to eat solid food, but they continue to use it to sleep and travel in until they are old enough to look after themselves.

Protecting the young

Brazilian Tapir

Camouflage pattern

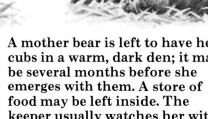

Malayan Sun Bear

Racoon

Most parents feed, clean and protect their babies. Some babies have a protective camouflage pattern; in the wild, it blends in with the natural vegetation and makes it difficult for other animals to see them.

A mother bear is left to have her cubs in a warm, dark den; it may be several months before she emerges with them. A store of food may be left inside. The keeper usually watches her with a hidden camera.

If young babies stray too far from the nest, the mother may pick them up by the scruff of the neck and carry them back. She may also carry them around if she is disturbed and wants to move them to a new nest site.

Growing up

Gorillas in zoos need to be kept in family groups. The young go everywhere with the adults and learn by watching and copying their behaviour. Young females learn how to look after babies by watching the mothers in their group. Female Gorillas that have been brought up on their own will not know how to care for a baby.

This is the male boss of the family. He is beating his chest to show that he is dominant (see page 22).

Young Gorillas have to learn what the body language and expressions of the adults mean.

Youngsters may form friendships by playing together. They will stay friends when they grow up.

Hand-rearing babies

This baby Orang-utan and Gorilla had to be reared by hand because their mothers did not know how to look after them.

Zoos try to leave young animals with their parents. However, if the mother cannot care for a baby, or the baby is sickly, orphaned, or one of a large litter, then the keeper has to look after it.

Rearing a baby is difficult, especially if it needs feeding every hour. Young hoofed animals are particularly difficult to rear, and usually die from infections. This is probably because they are not receiving substances, found in their mothers' milk, that would help them fight against illness.

A hand-reared baby that has lived with humans may refuse to mix with other animals. Therefore, as soon as a baby is capable of fending for itself, the keeper will put it back with members of its own species.

Baby Gorillas ride on their mothers' backs, holding onto her fur. This baby is learning what is good to eat by watching what her mother eats.

This youngster is learning to climb.

This female learnt from her mother how to hold her baby correctly.

Youngsters use their mouths to investigate strange objects.

Play

Leopard cubs

Learning how to fight.

When young animals play, they sometimes show adult behaviour, such as fighting, or running away from enemies.

Breeding and releasing rare animals

Some zoos are helping wildlife societies to save species threatened with extinction in the wild. They are acting as breeding centres for rare species and, where possible, are releasing zoo animals into the wild. However, releasing animals is never easy. The animals may not want to leave the company of humans and often cannot fend for themselves. They may have to be taught how to feed in the wild. The release area may also need to be protected or made into a reserve.

Keeping records

These Przewalski's Horses are from Marwell Zoo (G.B.). The species is thought to be almost extinct in the wild. When breeding such a rare species, a zoo has to be careful not to breed closely related animals such as mother and son, as this can result in sickly babies.

Each rare species has a stud book that records the ancestry and relationships of all animals in captivity. Zoos check with the stud book before they decide which animals to swap for breeding.

Operation Oryx

Stage 1

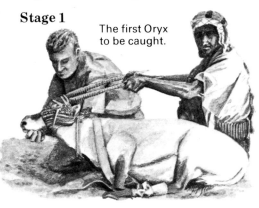

The first Oryx to be caught.

The Arabian Oryx used to be found throughout Arabia, but overhunting caused such a drop in numbers that by 1960, only a few were left. In 1962, Operation Oryx went ahead. The Fauna Preservation Society, backed by the World Wildlife Fund, sent out an expedition to Arabia and captured two males and one female. These animals were sent to Phoenix Zoo in Arizona (U.S.), where the climate is

Stage 2

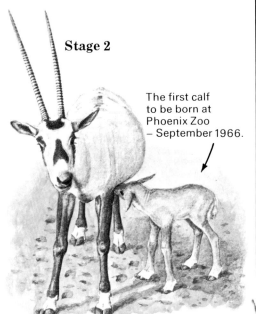

The first calf to be born at Phoenix Zoo – September 1966.

similar to that of Arabia. London Zoo (G.B.) then sent their single female Oryx to make up two pairs. These animals bred so well that there were soon enough Oryx to form a second herd at San Diego Zoo (U.S.).

Oryx live in large family groups with a top rank male.

Stage 3

Part of the **Arabian Oryx** herd at San Diego Zoo.

By 1978, there were several hundred animals in the zoo herds and it was decided that two family groups should be released into National Parks in Jordan and Israel. This was so successful that plans are now going ahead to release Oryx into Arabia; the release area will be guarded by local people.

The Né Né project

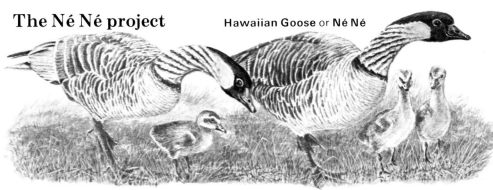

Hawaiian Goose or Né Né

In 1950 there were less than 50 Né Né left in the world. Five of these birds were sent to The Wildfowl Trust, Slimbridge (G.B.) to start a breeding group. Since then, the Trust has bred nearly 2,000 Né Né; this has helped to save the species from extinction.

In the 1960's, 200 of the birds were released in Hawaii (their native home). There were some problems at first, such as disease and nest disturbance by other animals, but now the geese have settled down and are breeding.

Saving the Giant Tortoise

The Galapagos Giant Tortoise was in danger of extinction, but now a National Park and a breeding centre have been created on one of the Galapagos Islands. Tortoises from the breeding centre are released into the park.

Honolulu Zoo (U.S.) is the other main breeding centre. It keeps its Tortoises in large, grassy enclosures, with muddy pools for them to sleep or relax in; this encourages breeding. The eggs are collected as they are laid. They are artificially incubated so that as many Tortoises as possible can be reared. The zoo also supplies other zoos with tortoises and could, if necessary, release some of its animals into the wild.

Breeding for conservation

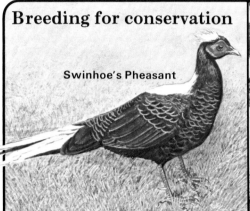

Swinhoe's Pheasant

European Eagle Owl chicks

The Pheasant Trust (G.B.) is helping to conserve rare species of pheasants by breeding and releasing them. Swinhoe's Pheasant has been successfully released into a forest reserve in Taiwan.

The Norfolk Wildlife Park (G.B.) has released a lot of its Eagle Owls into the forests of Sweden and Germany. Before the owls were released, they were taught to hunt in the wild.

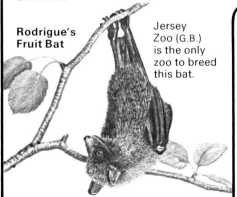

Rodrigue's Fruit Bat

Jersey Zoo (G.B.) is the only zoo to breed this bat.

Some zoos, such as Jersey Zoo, specialize in breeding particular species. If the wild populations of those species were to become extinct, zoo animals could be released into the wild to replace them.

Mud wallow.

Galapagos Giant Tortoise

Some special zoos

This is a Black Rhino from **Port Lympne Wildlife Sanctuary** (G.B.). The zoo has large groups of rare species such as Przewalski's Wild Horse, American Bison and Sable and Roan Antelopes. All the animals have a lot of space and freedom and breed well. Visitors can follow an expedition trail around the boundaries of the large paddocks.

This is a family of rare Spectacled Langurs from **Twycross Zoo** (G.B.). Twycross specializes in breeding apes and monkeys. It has breeding groups of many rare species such as Proboscis Monkeys and Black and White Colobus Monkeys. It also has family groups of Gorillas, Chimps and Orang-utans and lots of different species of gibbons.

The Norfolk Wildlife Trust (G.B.) specializes in breeding European species such as Badgers, deer, Arctic Foxes and the European Lynx in the photo above; it also breeds European waterfowl. By working with wildlife and conservation groups in Britain and Europe, it has managed to successfully release some of its animals into the wild.

These are Wood Bison from **Metro Toronto Zoo** (Canada). The zoo is divided into four main areas, each representing a different geographical area of the world. Each area has an expedition trail. On the Canadian trail, a silent electric train takes visitors through a long, wooded valley where there are animals such as Canadian Timber Wolves, Grizzly Bears and Wood Bison. The zoo is trying to release some of the Bison into protected areas in the wild.

Jersey Wildlife Preservation Trust (Channel Islands, G.B.) is a famous breeding centre for some of the world's rarest species, such as this Golden Lion Marmoset. Many of its animals have been sent to other zoos to start new breeding groups. The zoo has also helped to save two rare species – the Waldrapp Ibis and the Mauritius Pink Pigeon – from extinction. They have been bred in the zoo and will be released into the wild.

The Arizona-Sonara Desert Museum (U.S.) specializes in keeping desert animals from Arizona, such as this rare Arizona Ridge-nosed Rattlesnake, and the Desert Bighorn Sheep shown on the cover of this book. The animals are kept in enclosures that resemble their natural desert environments. There is a reptile and amphibian hall and an underground tunnel where nocturnal animals can be seen in their daytime hiding places.

The Wildfowl Trust, Slimbridge (G.B.) specializes in breeding rare species of waterfowl, such as these Chilean Flamingos from South America. It breeds many European waterfowl and acts as a natural breeding area for wild birds that are attracted to its large lakes.

Tama Zoological Park is a Japanese Zoo that keeps Asian animals, such as this rare Steller's Sea Eagle. The zoo has many native animals such as Japanese Macaque monkeys and Japanese Serows. It also has a special insect house which contains a Butterfly Farm and a Firefly Farm.

These are South American Bald-headed Uakaris from the **Miami Monkey Jungle Zoo** (U.S.). This zoo keeps different species of monkeys in a large area of tropical jungle. Most of the public walkway is enclosed with wire-netting so that the monkeys can move around freely.

This photo shows part of the African area of the **San Diego Wild Animal Park** (U.S.). The Park is linked to **San Diego Zoo**. Both places are enormous and together keep over a thousand different species. The Wild Animal Park has huge enclosures and breeds many rare species that you cannot see in other zoos. Scientists there are studying the

behaviour of each species so that more animals can be bred successfully.

The Park has a five mile (8 km) railway safari which runs through the African and Asian areas. San Diego Zoo has a 40 minute bus safari through part of the zoo and a cable car that carries visitors over the zoo so they can see down into the enclosures.

Taronga Zoo (Australia) has a very good collection of Australian animals. Most Australian mammals, such as this Cuscus, are nocturnal and are kept together in the nocturnal house. There are special houses for the Platypus and the Koalas, a large reptile house, and a tropical rainforest aviary for the Australian and New Guinea birds.

These two Sand Cats are from the Small Cat House at **Brookfield Zoo** (U.S.). Most small cats are semi-nocturnal, so the Cat House has special twilight lighting (see page 9). Each enclosure matches the cat's natural environment as closely as possible and special care is taken to keep the animals occupied. For example, the Sand Cats are kept in an artificial desert canyon; a sandy area in the "desert" is stocked with live insects for the cats to hunt.

This is **Boråsparken Zoo** (Sweden). All these African animals live together in one large enclosure. The photo on the cover, showing Elephants charging through the snow, is also from this zoo. The animals do not mind going out in the snow and can return to their heated sleeping quarters if 'they get too cold. The keepers are encouraged to spend a lot of time with their animals; you can see the ape keeper with her Chimps on the cover.

The LaFortune North American Living Museum is part of **Tulsa Zoo** (U.S.). It has four special buildings, each one representing a different climatic area.

This photo was taken in the Arctic/Tundra building and shows a Polar Bear swimming underwater. The building also has other Arctic animals, such as Snowy Owls and Arctic Foxes, as well as lots of interesting information about the people, geology and plant life of the area.

One of the attractions of **Topeka Zoo** (U.S.) is a special circular building containing a "tropical rain-forest". Mammals, birds and reptiles live in semi-natural conditions in the "forest". This building also has the largest waterfall in the state of Kansas.

Burgers Zoo and **Safari Park** (Netherlands) is famous for its Chimp colony. The chimps live in an outside enclosure which has trees for them to climb. The zoo also has 'a large African "savanna" enclosure which contains over 300 animals.

This Cheetah is from **Frankfurt Zoo**, which is one of the best zoos in West Germany. It provides good enclosures for its animals and breeds most of its species. There is a large nocturnal house and a reptile hall that contains a special "crocodile jungle".

Index

Books to read

Spotter's Guide to Zoo Animals. Rosamund Kidman Cox (Usborne). A handy pocket guide which will help you to identify the animals that you see in a zoo.
The Observer's Book of Zoo Animals. Jan Hatley (Fredrick Warne). A small and detailed identification book.
Life in the Zoo. Michael Chinery (Collins). Behind the scenes in a zoo. Lots of interesting photographs.
Doctor in the Zoo. Bruce Buchenholz (David & Charles). This book describes the daily life of a vet in an American Zoo. Lots of large photographs.
Animals on View. Anthony Smith (Weidenfeld & Nicolson). Detailed descriptions of most of the British zoos.
The Best of Friends. John Aspinall (MacMillan). An entertaining description of Howletts Zoo.
The Last Great Wild Beast Show. Bill Jordon and Stefan Ormrod (Constable). Describes why some zoos do not look after their animals properly.

Clubs and societies

Most zoos have clubs that you can join. A club will usually have its own zoo magazine and may organize film shows, lectures and special trips around the zoo. A club may also be able to help you with projects and will be able to give you ideas for things to do on a zoo visit.

Many zoos support conservation societies that are helping to protect animals in the wild. If you are interested in helping wild animals you could join the **Wildlife Youth Service**. This is part of the international **World Wildlife Fund**.

For membership details, send a stamped, self-addressed envelope to: Wildlife, Wallington, Surrey, Great Britain.
World Wildlife Fund, 60 St Clair Avenue East, Suite 201, Toronto 7, Ontario. M4T INS, Canada.
World Wildlife Fund Inc., 1319 18th NW, Washington DC 20036, U.S.A.
World Wildlife Fund, PO Box 58, 9 The Parade, Paekakariki, New Zealand; (This is also the address for Australia).

Photograph credits

We wish to thank the following zoos, organizations and individuals for all their help and for kindly lending us their photographs:

Arizona-Sonara Desert Museum, cover, 30; Berlin Zoo, 6; Bergen Aquarium, 10; Piers Bizony, 12; Borasparken, cover, 30; Brookfield Zoo (Rick Search), 31; Burgers Zoo/Safaripark, (Frans de Waal), 31; Frankfurt Zoo (roebuild: Ernst Müller), 9, 31; Howletts Zoo Park/Port Lympne Wildlife Sanctuary (Clive Boursnall), 6, 30; Jersey Wildlife Preservation Trust, Jersey, C.I. (Phillip Coffey), 5, 30; Geoffrey Kinns, 4; Marwell Zoological Park, 28; Metro Toronto Zoo, 30; Monkey Jungle, Miami, Florida, 31; Denis Moore, 18; Panaewa Zoo (James O. Juvik), 7; Royal Society for the Prevention of Cruelty to Animals, 5, 15; Royal Zoological Society of Scotland, 5; San Diego Zoo Photo, 17, 27, 31; Tama Zoological Park, 30; Taronga Zoo (H. Millen), 17, 31; Topeka Zoological Park, 31; Tulsa Zoological Park, 31; Twycross Zoo, 30; Vancouver Public Aquarium (Stefani I. Hewlett), 10; Philip Wayre, 5, 6, 29, 30; The Wildfowl Trust, Slimbridge, (J. B. Blossom), 5, 11, 30.

PRINTED IN BELGIUM BY

proost
INTERNATIONAL BOOK PRODUCTION